FINISHING LINE PRESS

www.finishinglinepress.com

Feral Ornamentals: Poems

by

Charlie Green

Finishing Line Press
Georgetown, Kentucky

Feral Ornamentals: Poems

ACKNOWLEDGMENTS

Publisher: Leah Huete de Maines
Editor: Christen Kincaid
Cover Art and Design: John Green
Author Photo: Charlotte Pass

Order online: www.finishinglinepress.com
also available on amazon.com

Author inquiries and mail orders:
Finishing Line Press
P. O. Box 1626
Georgetown, Kentucky 40324
U. S. A.

Table of Contents

I

II

III

IV

V

for Charlotte

I

Drowning

See me sink: a branch pulled under. How caught
I must look. The depth's invisible. I'm dead weight,

aged five. I walk the corrugated plank
into the lake, the water an opaque

brown, until the metal ends. In memory
the water whorls, my lungs become a sudden sea.

Even now, when I clench my arms
to my sides, my father's hands alarm

the skin of my armpits. He drags
me back to life, makes me unglug

the dirty lake I breathed. Today, a sip
goes down the wrong pipe,

and I am again just a system of bad
plumbing, a beating, breathing dud

despite my deaths. Forget the daily dawns,
I measure out last breaths, shattered moons,

each sequeled apocalypse, even the dream
where I'm pulled apart along a busted seam.

You can't live in the past, but still
you can die there. In the future, you will.

Akin

In White Sands many thousands of years ago, in the giant apostrophe of the giant
    sloth's footprint, our uncle's uncle's uncle put his own

small comma. He wielded an atlatl with a clovis-tipped spear to throw, and his
    calves and shoulders were taut bows ready to launch

the arrow of his body. The giant sloth he was tracking "ranged in size from
    something akin to a golf cart to the size of an elephant."

Our uncle wouldn't know either one—the hands we curl around the steering wheel
    parrot his hand gripped on the atlatl, ready to throw. In generations

someone will remember in their body that apostrophe and that comma, and put
    those marks on paper, and generations still after that, a British scientist,

whose English is a sibling to ours, will excavate those marks and tell us all a story.
    What the story can't tell is how our uncle knew the giant sloth: knew its
    movements, knew its mind, but failed to see its extinction

and our own. Our uncle had the patience to know the quarters and hackles of the
    animals that tracked in the muddy wake of Lake Otero,

the patience to let his body still itself into flora as he hunted, for hunting is waiting,
    learning how to know, so habit becomes foresight, a patience I try to learn

as I write myself into his genealogy, into his head, into his life. Maybe I can make
    my body taut like that, lose a tooth and think, "How can I use this?"

so every toy becomes a tool, and every tool a toy.

Flock

A flock
of birds this morning has
mastered drunken veer without
flapping, unmappable within
my windshield. They commute by

instinct
while I tread road behind
tires wobbling on a flatbed,
strapped down but looking dangerous
as any chaos. The birds

(I can't
identify them, as
unaware as any kid
distracted by the wilding life
out the window) know something

that we
never have, in a way we
never have, but who knows what
it might be. Behind this spattered
glass, I live my lovely myth

control,
my fingers tightly wrapped
around the rubber tightly
wrapped around a molded plastic
that's meant to bend in case of

a wreck.
I hope Saint Christopher,
patron saint of drivers, will
mind me. Assisi preached to birds,
his flock; I talk to myself,

depress
the brakes mid-talk to save
myself rear-ending someone
whose senses of space and time have
gone off for a morning lark,

I yell
at other drivers who
can't hear. Against my better
judgment, I transform into a
cursing screamer, scalding

myself
and my poor throat, thirty-
some-odd minutes from my job,
while the birds, that vast net wending,
wring from the air their being.

Self-Portrait as a Sand Mandala

I know it's right to be
       these sands, so moved
by hands toward an artful rest, the work

       of someone else's patience, and yet
the closer still
       I come to final shape, to meaning just

a moment before
       I'm brushed away, I pre-regret
the loss the monks will make

       of me. Why not
just let myself remain
       attached to myself, this moment,

the pouring funnels, a breath
       without the catch of doubt.
I do, until the colors rest

       then disappear, a harmony
displaced, becoming
       someone else's blessing.

Under Glass

Here we have a little man. You'll see
we've outfitted his terrarium
with everything he needs and thinks
he needs: a few books, outfits
he considers but rarely wears, a treadmill.

We used to give him WiFi and television,
but he became addicted and slept badly, often
during visiting hours. He enjoys coffee
with breakfast and lunch.
                                              Young man,
please don't tap the glass. He doesn't

like to be reminded that he's being
watched. And he can know—little men
have almost average human intelligence.
They cannot use tools with much
dexterity, but they can understand

and employ irony. This specimen was found
alone, sitting in the driver's seat
of a normal-sized car, a Ford Taurus,
reaching for the radio. We tried
to pair him with a mate, only

to discover that he felt alone with her,
and alone without. He told us
alone without was preferable. Calmer.
And in case you're worried that he finds
his treatment unbearable or hard,

we're pleased to say he doesn't.
When we first brought him here,
during our cleanings we'd find
his fingerprints had smudged the glass
the first few weeks, but since,

the glass stays clear. He's stopped
asking if we can set him free. He eats
the food that you can find
in our cafe, prepared by world-class chefs,
adjacent to the gift shop.

Inside

Through this window, I have two ways
to watch the snow fall. One: I track
a flake wending aimless until
it disappears behind the sill.

That doesn't last. There's too little
window. But I'm locked in here.
Also unsatisfactory:
to blur my vision, let the snow

pass as background noise, along with
the radiator clearing its throat,
the doors that, at some distance, close
and latch, the keys that jingle cold,

a misplaced laugh, steps trudging down
the hall (eighteen trips is one mile),
another patient arguing, and me,
listening to myself breathing.

Through this window, I have two ways
to watch the snow fall. One: I track
a flake wending aimless until
it disappears behind the sill.

That doesn't last. There's too little
window. But I'm locked in here.
Also unsatisfactory:
to blur my vision, let the snow

pass as background noise, along with
the radiator clearing its throat,
the doors that, at some distance, close
and latch, the keys that jingle cold,

a misplaced laugh, steps trudging down
the hall (eighteen trips is one mile),
another patient arguing, and me,
listening to myself breathing.

Morning Song

The automated deli slicer metronomes
the morning rituals: the coffee drop
that's drying on a rim, the scratched-out ink
of crossword guesses—~~clog~~ becoming "drip"

(turns out it's "leak"; the solver went and quit
with other puzzles harrying his mind)—
the toaster burning seeds that disengage
from bagels. Roosters still crow elsewhere, and

some denimed farmer made of dust, just like
us all, uncurls from bed all headachy
from birthing our nutrition out of soil
to underwhelming thank yous. Reveille

blares awake fatigued soldiers in lands
so far away or not. Alarms on phones
will wake us here. Students ruminate
on muffins, French declensions. Some are bronze

from tanning beds. I mask my jealousy
in judgment—I'm as white as any sclera
around an iris, invisible as hope
some of these days. I'm barely even there,

don't even register. They're in their lives.
Some have told me they cower from their futures,
which are vague and overbearing as a test's
directions. Some just hope to earn or secure

basic existences: apartments, pets,
a decent marriage. Between the now and then,
they'd like to build some memories that taste
of sugar, with a hint of salt, intense

and rising easily against the dark.
They don't imagine crosswords, furrows, meat
to slice for noontime crowds, the pre-dawn work,
the trumpet's bleary early-morning bleats.

They want it all, or just a safety net.
No hangnails, parking tickets, boredoms,
poetry, bread recipes that fail,
the sagging smiles, the blinking and the crumbs.

Process

The stovetop clicks and shishes. The eggs
wobble like turtles on their backs. *A watched*
pot never boils. —Grandmother. When
does cool water become room temp, and room warm?
Elsewhere, I wet the coffee grounds, let
them oxygenate, stir to release
their CO_2 (or so I've read), then fill.
In the pot, transparent balls, the seeds
of future boil, appear and disappear.
I assume in junior high or maybe
tenth-grade chemistry I learned
what happens, recited the three states
of matter so I can utter them now
in the kitchen, liquid solid gas, but
knowledge, for me, is a kind
of fairy tale. I've heard it, half-
forgotten it. My routines I know.
I check the water, because if it boils
too hard the eggs will crack. Now, some little
spheres of hot air rise to the top
like raptured souls. Not there yet.
If you listen long enough to wind chimes,
a melody will emerge, then disappear.
That's how forgotten knowledge works
for me. The trees outside are empty, then
release into the sky a murmuration of birds,
and then are empty again. That's how forgotten
knowledge works for me. A few pearls
blip at the bottom of the pot, nudging
the eggs, so I turn off the gas, lid
the pot. Thirteen minutes' rest. The time
it takes. I plunge the French press,
pour a cup, begin the day's forgetting. News,
sports, email. A student, who always writes
apart of instead of *a part of*, needs
an extension. I feel I should drop
the hammer, as a colleague says, but I don't

care enough this morning. *That's fine*, I write.
All best wishes. All of them. The timer
chimes. I drop an ice cube into a bowl
of water, spoon in the eggs to cool. Later,
I tap and roll them against the counter
and peel them, my thumbs untrained
for care. Chunks of white come with,
so the eggs I salt don't have those smooth
planes of shine. Instead they resemble
artifacts pocked by time, erosion, and
some clumsy novice archaeologist who,
untrained for care, begins the forgetting.

Winter Lesson

For whole minutes, the sun shone
unexpurgated
through the classroom
window. We could see
the parking meters mohawked
with snow. I was trying,
distracted, to explain time, how
we frame eras in retrospect
to ease our understanding, but
they were into the sun, as was I.
I wanted to tell them
this matters, because it does,
because it could help them
revise their lives or at least their hours,
but sunshine offered a glimpse
of past or future. And then the pills
of white came down again.

II

Improve Your Memory

Regret the error, then forget it. But if
you can't forget, dismember. The lie that wrecked
your marriage becomes a lily that you gave
to try and save it. Way back in a time

of *ers* and *ums*, you wrapped your hand around
the sun and saved some lives. Small ones, it's true,
but life is life, even if your hero
story requires some hemmings. Sally forth

along the narrow ledge, unhitched from fear,
as you tell of the time you waltzed with crisp slide steps,
the time the right words bloomed, the time you stopped
a looming blight, the time, the time, the time.

Recovery Room

Fluorescent lights and aging patients snooze.
My father sleeps, recovering. I've flown
from states away. His surgery was minor
but the first time either of my parents
has gone under the knife. A melanoma
on his face. My brother makes a joke; I laugh.
The doctor carved and scooped the cancer out
and grafted a patch of thigh onto his cheek.
We step into his room, and when I round
the bed, I see the gaudy stitches that fray
his face, the blood that stains his cheek, the sheet,
the pillow. My brother goes to sit with Mom.
I'm weak, my legs aphasic suddenly,
my mind gone faint. I stumble to a chair
by the door, facing the uncut cheek. The nurse
sees me sweating, pale enough in this
pale light to need attention. I don't want
to need attention. She brings me apple juice
in Styrofoam with pebbled balls of ice.
I sip embarrassed. Until we leave, I can't
stand up without a wobble. Out we go,
my brother joking about my weakness. My laugh's
a mask. My face is still inside that room
that we've just left, eyeing my father's cut
and grafted, bloody face, healing. Someday
he'll pass, and I will still be in that room,
ever the boy again, ever the son.

Sic Transit

"Pain is weakness leaving the body."
—U. S. Marine advertising slogan

The weakness is always leaving,
never arriving. The knot between
my spine and shoulder blade, the ache
of grief for some unrecoverable absence,

the marching orders from my head
to grill a memory or argument.
A childhood trauma, thought
forgotten, swells as it did back then.

My body is stitched from genetic threads,
synapses and oversights—a bomb forever
falling on soldier and civilian alike.

Unexpected Fireworks

Nighttime. My beagle, Cleo, is furled, fernlike,
        into herself. Outside, a firework claps
and to another room she bursts to hide

        under the furniture to nestle with
the dust. The window shows the far horizon:
        a celebration smokes the sky. But why?

Today's no holiday. A firework freck-
        les the dark, and then another, professional,
so dogs and soldiers scatter alike,

        amygdalas aflame. Their terror tunnels
to escape their bodies; finds no door; then mobs,
        while elsewhere children's irises contract

and pupils *ooh* their *aahs*. Birds, too, disor-
        ient. The startles send them to
their deaths. They strike our signage—STOP—windows,

        siding. Cartoons would circle stars around
their heads. I used to laugh, but now I've seen
        some dozen broken robin's eggs on side-

walks, blue as the name they made, a veined and dead
        precursor to what might have been. Instead,
they fell and cracked. They died before they lived.

        The birds that startle—they live a bit until
our shatter and our noise deflate them. Long
        ago, the second-century Chinese

wrote on green bamboo and roasted the stalks
        to dry. The wood would pop and scare off threats.
Later, centuries, fireworks were born

and begat gunpowder weaponry. The burst
of joy created suffering. So
      it goes. Shaved metal salts explode as colors:

red is strontium, copper is blue. The salt
      that dusts your steak burns yellow, if you like.
Carcinogens delight and fall. The cows

      across the field tonight aren't spooked, thank god,
unlike the ones in Maine, Ohio, Mar-
      yland who burst into stampedes. Enthralled,

I watch, detached from what they celebrate
      tonight, however many miles away,
my borrowed awe a celebration I

      don't mind confessing that I want to keep.
The sky is silent now. The smoke migrates
      into dark. The quiet tells me I should sleep.

Interrogative

No, where are you
from? What elsewhere?

       Derivations, please:
       how soft-soiled

the banks, what men
-ace thrust you from

       the home you didn't know
       you knew so well, the wind,

the way grass shoots
through concrete and asphalt

       no matter how tightly packed.
       Why did they send you

away? What did they send you
toward? Whose tongue is clumsy

       in your mouth? Mine swells
       when I'm in trouble, so you

must be in trouble. Was it
encoded when the ovum

       became a home for itself
       and another? Or before

a single cell divided to
jump-start the world?

       What word was first? What word
       was first? What word? What word?

Hunger Stones

"When you see me, weep."
—Inscription on an Elbe River stone usually below the water line

Drought starved the river. Unexploded bombs
from prior wars emerged. We rubbed our fingers
on the rust and tasted flecks against our thumbs.
They tasted of blood. We left the tense or dead
munitions to themselves. The water level
lowered still, and old words surfaced. Our people,
long forgotten, had left a note:
you will survive until you don't.

Most Human Knowledge

I'm told in certain herds the boldest deer
venture the furthest forward foraging
and die as a result—there, predators
lie waiting. The timidest, with skitters in
their blood and brains, hang back and starve to death.
And in some middle range of bravery
are those who scrounge and forage to survive
just lean enough to run to safety. Who knows
if this is true. Just like most human knowledge,
it has a moral if you tilt it a certain
way. It's Goldilocks: too hot, too cold,
just right, now go and do your homework, change
the sheets, clean up your mess, and by the way
stop crying all the time. We resist our moral
ends but sometimes want them all the same.
I am the deer that's hanging back, no feast
of berries, no flesh that's ripe to eat, the only
flavor in my mouth the unnutritious
grass and evergreens and twigs and tongue.

The Gallery of Dancers

Offstage eternally, limbs stretched and ready,
watched when they're not being watched, the dance
off canvas but before their eyes—they see
so much I don't. There's very little chance
these marks will mark my memory.
                                                    We squeeze
our coats and scarves. The placard on the wall
tells us this painting took four days. Four days
of brushstrokes, stepping back, re-seeing. With all
of that, I'm past in seconds.
                                        "Duality,"
some man says. "It's all about duality."
Someone's read the placard, too. His wife
or daughter (hard to tell) walks on. Cezanne
bores her and her Hermès scarf. I yawn.
I try to stifle it.
                        Up next: still life.

Glacial Erratics

Misshapen boulders, placed
precarious and drifted without a say,
striated by time and vanished
surroundings, these common outsiders
tell the landscape, *This is what
you're not.* They make the space
around them. Ice abraded,
eroded, stole them, stowed them,
and now we awe and, from the composition
that wandered south, can trace
the glacier's path right back
to its origin. *Here was birth,* they say,
*the beginning after the beginning
after the beginning before that.*

The End of the Line

The butterfly that flaps its wings
                and, half a world away, incites
a hurricane? A myth, most like-
                ly spread by the *lepidoptera.*
But sturdy research shows that sperm
                can carry on some unknown traits
of dad's behavior. Not just the gene,
                but state of mind, anxiety,
that sugar tooth that sneaks a do-
                nut: they thrive and hitch your secrecy
into your child. The tantrum that
                you threw, the hate you swallowed deep,
the way grief knit itself into
                your bones, the hunt of fathers miles
and years removed: you pass these on.
                Nucleotides: CGAT,
as well as alphabets and signs
                that stow aboard during the trek
within the epididymis—
                the coiled six-meter tube where sperm
mature (though, fittingly, they reach
                their full maturity inside
the egg). We know the English al-
                phabet, but we don't know the veiled
characteristics riding with
                our DNA. You pass these on.
And I admit: I'm glad I won't.
                No echo of my errors learns
to walk, requiring my hands
                to button up a coat or dial
a late-night bail bondsman to drag
                an angry, too-smart asshole out
of jail. I drove my father's car
                into a neighbor's pond once, lied
about the flooded engine, mud-
                dy floor mats, where I'd been the night
before. Thank God that lie won't boom-

erang. But then again, I'll miss
the echo of my voice, the me
         that finds itself in undiscovered
possibility. I'll end my days
         with strangers, if I'm lucky enough
to live beyond my memories.
         My spine will curl, the hand that brings
my spoon up to my lips will have
         its own genetics, a father who
was cruel, or kind, or both, and did
         not know the breaths he took were full
of information that we still
         don't understand, that every act
he undertook tutored the hand
         that, in the end, might steady mine.

III

Body and Soul

We think we name the river by
its water, but we don't. The water
only ever goes, as do the edges,
the mud and silt and soil and clay.
Those shift, but slow, like rusting tanks.
We name the river by its banks.

A Ways

We decided it was time to move
the mountain. We all approved;
we were not arrogant. It was no
bigger in our heads than a snow
flake. Once, we saw a pigeon heave

bread with a skin-flap of ham grooved
to its underside, until it removed
itself to the ground. And so
we decided it was time,

and though some disapprove,
we've just begun to improve
the landscape—there's still a ways to go.
We don't regret the loss of lives, the slow
build to anger that you've
finally voiced. We decided it was time.

Oh, Christ

—after "The Windhover"

I am this morning morning's moodbound weak-
  ling, duke of doldrums, unextincted dodo,
  forever riding gravity's flat earth, an unmissed link
that's striding low, thought "fat and clumsy," but well-adapted
to my unecstatic environment. Now off, rebuffed by wind,
  my heart in hiding, heeling, unstirred by word or beak,
  I take my waking slow. My wimpling wing is bent.
That's my achievement: mastery of nothing.

But as the sun's sheer plod re-echoes through
  the window, fire breaks free. I am resilient,
I'm springing back, my buckle straightens to

  the taut-bowed spine of wonder. Light beats brilliant
against the floor, a gold-vermilion view
  of what might be: one life, one pair, one billion.

Babel

I'm listening in at one end
of where they're building the tower:
miles and miles away
from the other. The engineers
realized that to reach my Heaven,
they'd need a miles-long elliptical
foundation. They're laying
it now, miles and miles
and miles. The overseer—not me,
but of the project—is at the end
I'm observing. He's set up a system
for communicating along the line
from his end to the other: instead
of running messengers back
and forth, they have lines of men
who repeat messages down the line
and back. Good thing they don't
have runners—they don't know
the future holds Pheidippides, who will
run from Marathon to Athens to announce
Athenian victory, then die, according
to the story. They don't know the legend
of Pheidippides will inspire a race
in his honor. But their line of message-
senders will fail. It's like the game
of telephone, centuries away, even past
the invention and extinction of the telephone,
but if I were to announce
myself and tell them
about the telephone, they'd shit themselves
or burn an effigy of me. So I giggle
to myself and listen. "'Free,' I said, not
'friend.' I don't know how he heard that."
The overseer's on a rant, again. There's
management for you, I want to tell him,
but I don't. It's lonely knowing everything.
They think they want to reach me, they

think they want to know. But if they knew,
they wouldn't want to know. In the end,
an undetected crack in the foundation
will bring down their tower. They'll
blame me, because they don't know. I'm
the one who split their voices, they'll claim,
because they won't hear how much their voices split
as their words run rampant down the line, words
climbing from all fours to their hind legs, much
like these people did over eons, becoming human.

Aphasia

Among the words that trek across
the region named for Broca, one
is lost. I look around the class
-room as if it will appear. I mind
the students minding me. I have
to move on. I say, *Sorry, aphasia*
(at least I know that word) and put
the lesson back on its path until,
voilà, the word arrives, my scalp
relaxes, and discussion is
derailed again to celebrate
this little win, until the next
time a word is lost awhile, or for good.

The Drowned Man

I was Pharaoh's fastest. When Moses led
the senseless run toward the waters, I pulled
the reins to slow my horses. But then the sea
diverged itself into two walls and stood
as if held by glass. I whipped my pair to speed.
They trusted me. The earth their hooves unearthed
flew past my ears. The water-walls were miracle
enough. But the path was dry. On either side,
fish swam through the walls as if escaping some
unholy birth canal. Some carried over
into the other water, others hit
my horses' flanks and left a fleeting stamp
of magic water. One landed by my foot.
I let it ride co-captain of my chariot.
Some fell into the sand and flopped for their lives.
Behind, I heard my countrymen yelling
and whipping, their horses clapping on the bone-
hard bottom of the sea, and when I saw
the far edges of the waters and Moses' hand
upraised, I saw the future: Moses' waves
would drown us with our horses in unsettled graves.
I called and waved to them *Retreat!* but they
kept charging. My only hope was reaching shore
before the waters drowned me, closing behind
the dirty footsoles of the runners. Life
was on that shore. I couldn't save my men.
I could only save myself. My horses flagged,
unused to such long fervor. The last man cleared
the water. I heard him shout, "We're free, we're free!"
As Moses' hand began its fall, I reached
out my hand as if to hold his up by faith
or magic. To no avail. The waters fell
back into one and took my horses and
my chariot. I flew forward toward
the water and shouted, before it swelled my mouth,
"I believe!" The waters swallowed me. I flailed,
and I kept shouting even though the water

was choking me, and I could feel the tears
bursting from my eyes, even in that sea,
and as I realized that I was dying
and somehow at peace with that, the muddy bottom
brushed my toes, my arms were righting me,
and I found footing. I stood and infant-walked
until my head arose above the water.
I coughed out cups of it, bitter with salt
and sand. I wracked my body onto shore
and fell. My breath returned to me. I swept
the blur away from my eyes, I saw their free
heads bob on the horizon. I tried to call,
but my voice still drowned along the wind. Behind,
some spokes and spears were floating. We, the we
that I had known, were gone, and now I had
become a man without a people.

Nest

Their pairs of eyes bobbed opalescent
as speckled life. The birdlets, winged
but featherless, rasped wild with hunger.
Lined by twigs and candy wrappers
dropped by the college kids who traipsed
our sidewalk from dorm to bar, their lives
ahead, the nest rested atop
our hedge. Their mother sat, close-winged,
a tree away. My wife and I stood still
to awe. Weeks later, the birds were gone.
The nest remained. This winter, a box
of Keystone Light sat upside down
atop the nest atop our hedge.
I tossed it in the recycling,
then scraped de-icing salt from my boot
with fraying laces and overheard
the tipsy students stumbling by.
They spill their pleasures. I hoard mine.

IV

A Clown of Sonnets

*The clown shall make them laugh
that are tickled in the lungs.*
　　　　　　—Shakespeare, *Hamlet*

i.

All seven of us fold inside the car,
our limbs and flowers wrinkled and uncouth.
We're geared for joy, our tears and losses far
away. We have no interest in the truth
beyond the laugh. We know we're cloying
and necessary, the peasants whose low status
and slapstick pains dissolve the sadness
of the nobles, raise up those cowboying
around the barrels, wash the gloss of wisdom
on each well-educated fool. Our shoes
will make you feel you're so right-sized, victim
of fate's rank and shitty whims. *Amuse,
buffoon!* We turn the key, accelerate,
swallow down our pasts, and out we skate.

ii.

We swallow down our pasts, and out we skate
to slip, roll, fizzle, twirl, and juggle
our balls and bodies and jokes, communicate
in the broadest possible gestures
that we can live and laugh, so that struggle
can be shoved aside by common jesters
who move elusive and invertebrate,
in pain but free from suffering, who shuffle
in and out of trouble, wander figure-eight
into the pie in the face, who lecture
via three-ball flash and rebut with seltzer
and wish our jokes would accumulate
and squat in cochlea and, later, haggle
with your brain to say, life is light conjecture.

iii.

"For your brain to say, 'Life is light conjecture,'
you must be a fool." Okay, a valid
point, but still, the crumbling architecture
we call wisdom pales against the pallid
whiteface of the charming, charmed buffoon.
Yes, you'll dismiss me as some halfwit Bozo
whose wealth's in vanishing laughs, a tycoon
whose salad fork is just a blown balloon.
Oh, please. "At least the acrobats have skill,"
you say, "at least they're not the ill-bred hacks
who pull out rainbow handkerchiefs until
the cliché dies a second death. All facts."
Cliché? No skill? All facts? I mean—ill-bred?
You stupid halfwit bastard judge, my mother was a royal, my father was a
        learnèd man with robes and nth degrees, they lived until they
        couldn't. Now, like you, they're dead.

iv.

And when they couldn't live, my folks, they died.
Please, when I die, I'd like to be buried
in full costume: the wig, the oversized
shoes and facepaint and ruffled suit. I need
my casket to look like Aladdin's shoe:
upturned at the end. Go out with a laugh,
I tell myself. I'd like the laughs to corkscrew
throughout the parlor. Friends should see me off
without a tear, not even one they've painted.
My parents' funeral was dire, no jokes
or joy in the receiving line. I fainted.
I'll never live it down, so someone coax
the life out of my death. The harlequins
should tumble for your death-defying grins.

v.

The harlequins should tumble, for your death
will not defy the odds, and grins will stamp
themselves on faces day-to-day. Your breath
will catch. Your heart will stop. And on the tramp
will go, abundantly, and the Auguste,
his patterns unaligned, his circus ring
his home where pranks are art and no *mot's juste*,
will show that laughter is worth worshiping.
No, God is not a clown, and Pagliacci
wears the face I note each night before
I go to bed. No heaven I can see
for clowns or lion tamers. God's a bore.
His repertoire's the same old sleight-of-hand
that made you think the sky's a holy land.

vi.

What made you think the sky's a holy land
is gravity. When acrobats muscle
their bodies beyond its hold, the minute hand
moves back to join the hour in prayer. Wrestle
with that angel, the right to fall without
a net. The man who swallows fire spits
it back toward the big top's peak, airs out
his faith in flame. You shouldn't trust his kiss.
I used to watch from behind the curtains, dolt
that I was, and awe at practiced tricks. But now
I check my paint and give myself a jolt
from a toy buzzer. I arch my eyebrow
and honk my nose. Hey, even Jesus knew
to con the crowd you have to pull a trick or two.

vii.

To con the crowd, you pull a trick or two.
To con yourself, you have to think you're not
the fool. The flea-bit wisdom you accrue
is just some self-fulfilling, scattershot
regression to the mean, distracted self
you wish you'd shed. Bah. Let me tell a joke.
Some folks are scared of clowns. Their ears are deaf
to age-old humor. Maybe laughter's broken.
I guess it's not that funny. In life, so far,
I've found that everything I know is wrong.
The expiration dates are sneaking closer.
Before the cue: my body's *adios*
will overspeak my dreams. They played our song—
all seven of us fold inside the car.

V

Ornamental

Their buds bloom early in spring,
so universities and cities gird
their walkways with the Bradford Pear.
Depending on the nose, they're redolent
of rotten fish, a sun-baked dumpster, or
a wafting post-coital afternoon. Once spring
sets down its roots, these trees
deposit white petals along sidewalks
like community-theater snow. The fruit's
inedible for us. By the time they're old
enough to drink, they brittle
and vee, their weak forks impeding
our footfalls on the crackled concrete. Despite
its frailty, *pyrus calleryana*, imported cultivar,
pirates the soil from sea to salty sea.
This feral ornamental is nature best
seen through windows, fittingly, because
nature now, for most, is neither smelled
nor felt. In warm autumns, their leaves
bloody up the sky. In winter, the trees
reset themselves for next year's stink.

Discovery

We had mixed feelings about discovering
new sins. Adrenaline, we later saw,
had flooded us. But in the moment, hot
with pleasure, then hot with shame, some took their names
off the project. Thus, more of us could profit.
We filed the patent paperwork in hopes
the money would roll in. We also had
our noble motives—that any time of day
some strangers somewhere would be pleasuring,
thanks to our work. Sure, they'd feel shame, but no
good comes without a cost. Then we learned that we
were late to the game, just like the man who tried
to patent happiness. Public domain
had absorbed our sins. We stood to gain nothing
but grief. All that lab time, the protocols,
the happy accidents, the data, graphs
and charts and arguments, the double-blind
testing, the late-night drinking, the affairs, the smug,
pure love of discovery, was all for naught.
No peer review, no honor from our peers.
Only the shame of being dumb enough
to learn again what the world already knew.
Turns out the Germans had a word for it.
We humbled. We sobered up—well, most of us—
and returned to quiet work with little hope
of making names or even coming flush
against the heat of new discovery.
One night, we found ourselves together, laughed
at our embarrassment. It felt like closure.
Then, late into the night, we fell into
a really new discovery. We slicked
it with our wits, we circled it and drew
out schema for our pleasures and our shames,
and knew that we were on to something big.
We didn't know if it was undiscovered.
We walked for weeks close-mouthed and grinning dumbly.
We were numb with joy, and we decided

that we would keep this joying to ourselves:
Let other people pave their roads to hells.

The Garbage Man

His bones are copper stolen from
            construction sites, his tendons bands
that wrapped asparagus. He lifts
            his forearm to smell the echo. There is
so much to taste, so much to love.
            When he drinks, the liquid trills the ridges
of the water bottle—his thorax—and settles
            into a different plastic (Clorox,

polyethylene). He wishes
            for a home on the Pacific that's washed
with gentle waves. His life is epic
            in his dreams, the spotlight jaunty on
his foil skin. Love calls to him
            from cars and open windows. He sees
it in the hands that interlace.
            One pulls the other through a crowd.
One time, he heard that love is all
            you need. So that is what he wants

to find, to make himself complete
            as us. Sometimes, he swaps the springs
that are his knees for crunched aluminum
            still sloshing hidden sugared rills.
He'd love to love, but he's alone.
            Sometimes, under the right streetlamp,
his shadow makes him look just like
            a man kissing his wife goodnight.

Peking Man

Did you exist? Were you a person?
Did love or one of its cousins ever
embrace you? Seven or eight hundred
thousand years ago, you lived,
say the remains, and died. Your calvaria—

your brain's bone ceiling—remained, were re-
discovered. You would become a link,
which few become. In the 1920s
Davidson Black, Canadian, found
you, named you, took a tooth to keep

in a locket, gold, on his watch chain.
He was known to examine teeth late
into the night. Back then, Piltdown Man
still echoed, the missing link, only
suspected as a hoax. Decades passed

before it was exposed. Pierre Teilhard
de Chardin, the Jesuit philosopher who found
a Piltdown tooth, who urges us toward
Omega Point, helped find you, too. But
you were real, and you existed

again. At first, you were not thought
to be a man: *Sinanthropus pekinensis,*
as named by Black, before you were,
it was agreed, *homo erectus.*
What was your name? Did you have

a name? Did you see your reflection
in the water, did you grunt or say
the knot of sounds your family said
when they needed your attention?
The Peking man was a thinking being,

standing erect, dating to the beginning
of the Ice Age. Like all of us, you were
forgotten. And, like us, you were many:
fragments from multiple bodies. Found
in Zhoukoudian and removed. In 1941,

amid one local occupation, amid
the start of worldwide war, you were boxed
in cotton by U. S. Marines. Somewhere
between that boxing and the running
aground of the SS President Harrison,

you disappeared. The casts remain.
The remains do not. They molder
in the sea, or were buried, or were
dug up in the construction of now-
dilapidated buildings. You've died

more deaths than most of us. I'll be
cremated. I'd like my ashes spread
to any winds that take them. Maybe
in several hundred thousand years
or so, some chemical test will reveal

to whom- or whatever cares to look
that I existed, a notch in the universe's
Domesday Book. Who writes us all?
So primitive, they will say. Yes, he had
language, and also thought, and he

could start a fire, but only with
a lighter or help. He didn't know
so much, not even how to feel
at ease with people or himself.
He thought of the body as apart

from everything else. I envy you
a thing you never knew and never
would care to know—your place in us,
the mystery around your bones,
how love evolves into a home.

Anatomy Lesson

When desire climbs a male giraffe, seizes
his genitals, and periscopes up to
his inclined neck, evolution says
to taste another's urine. Often, that
means arching back his neck, then headbutting
another giraffe in the bladder until

a stream releases. To taste the urine, the male
giraffe exhibits what is called the flehmen
response. *Flay*men, it's pronounced, an echo
of the violence of the initial amorous
assault, and comes from a German word (it's true,
they have a word for everything) that means

to look spiteful. To love in spite. Now, once
the giraffe has tasted the forced excretion,
he decides whether or not to mount. *Decide,*
in this context, is etymologically rich, coming
from *de-*, meaning *off*, and *caedere*, to cut.
Such complex evolution must be fine-

tuned, you'd think, but between 75
and 95 percent of the time, the male
giraffe's impulse is errant, so much so
that males are mounting other males. Or maybe
we've got it wrong, and the giraffe has cottoned on
to the fact that we are watching. It's all for show.

Hey, who could blame me, he thinks, holding up
his front hooves. *Blame Darwin, et alia.*
Evolution made me this way. Instinct
overpowers the giraffe, so he
then overpowers. Instinct, after all,
derives from *in-* and *stinguere*—to prick.

Chiropractice

Relax, he says. Instead, my muscles stand
in protest, tendons tense, my vertebrae
engage their locks. Face down, my cheeks against
a roll of paper that chatters every time
he asks me to adjust or else adjusts
me himself, I can't relax. I never was
in any lax, so I can't re-. I know

the pain is coming, faster than a thought,
and leaving faster than adrenaline's
escape. He'll shove his hands against my back.
He's done it many times before. I keep
returning, mainly because my spine's a rope
that's kinked all wrong. Relief will come, I know,
and yet I can't feel unafraid of the pain
that disappears as quick as it arrives.
(Not with that attitude, I sometimes joke.)
I'd like to be the good patient, the one
whose tension dissipates the moment Doc
intones Relax, the one who cracks each time

he works his hands. I want to be so good
my spine aligns and stays that way. I'll stand
up straight and never hurt, and never need
another's hands to fix whatever's wrong.
But my body's not alone. It needs distinct

articulation from another, one

whose force unfuses me from agony.

Regulatory Bodies

In 1980, smallpox died for good,
according to authorities. Rightly,

no one has laid a wreath. But smallpox was
a character, a missionary, us:

The Crusades spread that virus vast across
the European continent just as

the Portuguese brought smallpox to the west
of Africa. The slave trade, the Puritans,

the British ships down under: each colony
remade the landscape of human flesh, until

a Brit, Edward Jenner, shot cowpox into
a child. People were dying, so he thought to fill

a needle with a milkmaid's pus (her hands
were poxed, the rest of her unblemished) and put

it into little Phipps. The boy survived.
Now vaccination had a name. It spread.

Long after, British soldiers at Fort Pitt
gave blankets to the natives, laced with strains

of *Variola major*. Afterward,
it hid away in civil wars, pursued

by needles. A year after my birth, it died.
Let's mourn our anti-hero now: it's dead

except for traces still in vials in two
known places, maybe elsewhere for all we know:

it turns out cowpox likely wasn't our
protector. Horsepox was. So *equination*

just might serve us better. Meanwhile, smallpox
is waiting for its curtain call of loud

applause. It's not all dead. No—nothing is.
Instead, it's living in a quiet pause.

Lullaby

The quiet never curls
around my sleep. The blanket
needles as if my skin's a vinyl record,
my breath elapses in rasps,
I murder all the counted
sheep. The quiet never curls around
my sleep. My ear's a swelling net

trapping sound. Against the roof, branches
rehearse their clodding blocking
and gossip about the wrong
I did this afternoon, the too-quick
smirk, the look away,
the wrong not yet undone.
Long past tomorrow, guilt
will swell and keep. The quiet

never curls around
my sleep. And far beyond,
the sun reflects its joy against
the moon and through my window. I roll
and kick. The blanket is
a mossy, humid heap.
No matter what I do, the
quiet never curls

around my sleep. Between
my toes, a steam escapes, an itch
frisks my scalp, I craft a fantasy
of articulate apologies, my voice folded
into contrition. I try not
to think how meanwhile, elsewhere,
a housekeeper knocks and hopes
the guest has gone and left
a five or ten folded under
the remote, how for many someones
apnea rattles their sleep and curdles

their dreams. If I ever
had a strength, it's somewhere
deep beneath. I'll dig until
a skinny root invites me down in to the dirt,
until the *quiet never*

curls around my sleep.

Acknowledgments

"Drowning"—*The Missouri Review Online*

"Akin"—*Tar River Poetry*

"Under Glass"—*The Gateway Review*

"The Drowned Man"—This work originally appeared in *Image*. Reprinted with permission.

"A Clown of Sonnets"—section v. appears in *Measure Review* as "Sock and Buskin"

Thanks to Leah Maines, Christen Kincaid, and the staff at Finishing Line Press for their generosity in helping me put this into the world. Thanks to Speer Morgan, Luke Whisnant, Joe Baumann, and Shane McCrae for seeing life in some of these poems. Thanks to my colleagues in the Department of Literatures in English at Cornell University for their support and friendship, especially Stuart Davis and Roger Gilbert. Thanks to Mukoma Wa Ngugi, Catherine Pierce, and Jillian Weise for giving their time and endorsement to this collection.

I am lucky to have crossed paths with extraordinary writers and teachers from high school through my job, at the University of Arkansas at Little Rock, the University of Missouri, the University of Cincinnati, and Cornell University. Thank you all for tolerating my jokes and drafts, and for your care and encouragement.

Thanks to my parents, who had the bad but useful sense to indulge my interests in reading and writing. If anyone discovers the way to thank parents in a way commensurate with what they've given, please let me know. Thanks to my brother Jim, who inspires me in gratitude, warmth, and creativity. And thank to my brother John, who has always pushed me to sharper thought and greater play, and who designed the perfect cover for the book.

With the greatest gratitude to Nick Friedman for his patience, enthusiasm, silliness, and care. I owe you for so much of whatever is good here.

And to Charlotte, my essential, for everything.

Born and raised in Arkansas, **Charlie Green** earned his M.A. in English at the University of Missouri and his Ph.D. at the University of Cincinnati. Since 2010, he has taught writing in the Department of English at Cornell University. His poems have appeared or are forthcoming in *Image Journal, The Missouri Review Online,* and other venues. His fiction and essays have appeared in *Another Chicago Magazine, The Southeast Review,* and other journals. *Feral Ornamentals* is his first book.

www.ingramcontent.com/pod-product-compliance
Lightning Source LLC
Chambersburg PA
CBHW021159090426
42740CB00008B/1156